PLAYWRITING
A SHORT STEP-BY-STEP GROUP-ORIENTED UNIT

BY ROBIN L. SNOVER

ART BY TERRA SNOVER

ISBN: 978-1-300-73313-3

DEDICATION

This book is affectionately dedicated to all the students who worked through this playwriting process, wrote and produced wonderful one-act plays, and spurred me on to share these ideas with other students and their teachers. It is also dedicated to my loving and supportive family who hung with me through the many drafts of this book.

CONTENTS

PART ONE
TEACHER INTRODUCTION

TEACHER INTRODUCTION

This project is based on the philosophy of progressive thought. It rests on the theory that the visual and performing arts can greatly aid learning when combined with more traditional subject areas. The type of learning proposed involves creative self and group learning and the improvement of useful skills as a result of the experience. Students are given the opportunity to develop a one-act play whose content is in an area of their own choosing; research into self-chosen content often progresses naturally. The process involves using and improving a wide variety of language arts and dramatic arts skills and the product is a project that can be of immediate use, if desired.

This playwriting unit is written with the needs of the transescent learner kept in mind. It specifically caters to the adolescent student's needs for high levels of peer interaction, search for understanding, social-emotional characteristics, activities that are of personal interest to the learner, and require a wide variety of intellectual skills. This unit can be one part of a full exploratory drama or language arts curriculum.

Students are dealing with an ever-increasing highly technological information-oriented society and will need to understand the dynamics of communication and human relations and be versed in the skills of both. They will need to think divergently about problems and explore creative solutions. They also need help developing into self-aware individuals who are confident in their unlimited human potential. They must be guided into becoming self-directed learners who are responsive to change and how to work with it.

This unit is written up in the Tylerian Model for creating curriculum designs; it contains elements of objectives, activities, organization of activities, and evaluation. Objectives are organized sequentially and are interrelated. Evaluation has been designed to determine whether objectives are being obtained. The design also utilizes the process-concept structure. This format combines the teaching of concepts such as brainstorming, character, scenario, and editing. It then designs activities that reinforce the concepts through processes such as generating germinal ideas individually and in large groups, creating characters, writing up a play outline, and oral group play reading/editing sessions. It allows for limited direct transferring of information to students and unlimited potential for pupil participation. This design also incorporates elements of humane education in that it encourages students to display an interest in others, in having success, in evaluating cooperatively, in inquiring and discovering, and in working closely with others. It combines intellectual, emotional, social, and aesthetic development.

Evaluation design for this project evolves around a combination of traditional and naturalistic processes. Conceptual growth can easily be measured through quizzes as well as students' abilities to correctly fill out character and scenario worksheets. Examination of the students' play drafts as well as the finished one-act play can be compared with previously written materials to measure improvement in writing skills. Informal data collection will also be used by inquiring from students, other faculty, and parents as to improvements and success of the program's objectives. Formal post-unit student evaluations can be administered and evaluated. Many other successful types of evaluation techniques could be used, such as video recording or having skilled observers charting skills in brainstorming fluency and flexibility progress. Care must be taken that the evaluation processes used fit in with the curriculum naturally and do not bog it down needlessly. Therefore, I propose that evaluation mainly be limited to quizzes, informal evaluation of the process by the teacher and skilled outside observers, and informal post-unit course evaluations done by students.

If students, skilled observers, or the instructor find that changes in the program are needed, it would be best for the teacher, author of the curriculum, or a well-trained drama instructor to solve the problem. A coalition of the above might also prove beneficial if more objectivity is required or desired. The latter may prove useful in determining where change is needed. Curriculum of this sort is a multi-facet issue and the change could be needed in how the curriculum is delivered, the way students are grouped, or within the curriculum design itself. In order that this unit be most useful, I am including a unit outline, instructional information and materials, evaluation sheets, and two plays that have resulted from this process. You and your students may adapt these plays, use them as guidelines or utilize your creative abilities and make your own one-act.

If this design were adopted into either exploratory drama courses or language arts programs I feel, if used properly, you would experience much of what I have already discovered through the piloting stages of its development. Socially students would be learning how to think, communicate, negotiate, and change their ideas with authority figures and small and large groups of their peers. Politically students would be learning elements of good citizenship; they would need to go with the group's decisions, after having discussed and decided on ideas, and try and work at creating the best possible result of the decisions. Culturally students would be exploring an art form that is thousands of years old and still vital today. Most importantly, however, learners would more than likely be motivated and enjoy creating their own, producible one-act. The excitement escalates if they get to go on and perform it.

OBJECTIVES

1. Understand playwriting concepts and vocabulary.

2. Brainstorm original ideas relevant to a playwriting project.

3. Process thoughts into words, phrases, sentences, outlines, and dialogue.

4. Verbally and literally share ideas with others.

5. Listen to and reflect on others' ideas.

6. Verbally and literally evaluate ideas based on criteria.

7. Negotiate through group decision-making processes.

8. Problem-solve individually, in small, and large groups.

9. Formulate and ask questions for clarification.

10. Make group decisions and stick with outcomes.

11. Record group decisions in an organized format.

12. Create titles, settings, characters, plot and dialogue based on a germinal idea.

13. Orally interpret a script from a character and playwright's point of view.

14. Edit illogical thoughts, actions, grammar, spelling, and punctuation.

15. Manage time appropriately and stick to deadlines.

16. Explore creative self-growth and the joy of creating with others.

ACTIVITIES

1. Read workbook, discuss concepts, and provide oral and written examples, when necessary.

2. Keep a notebook with notes, vocabulary list, worksheets, workbook, quizzes and other class materials.

3. Think up germinal ideas for a class one-act play, that takes place in one setting in 20 to 30 minutes.

4. Write down ideas in workbooks and then verbally share and evaluate these ideas with other class members.

5. Verbally express personal opinions concerning worth and interest of developing project with the class as a whole.

6. Sort ideas into play criteria categories and write these down as a group and individually in workbooks.

7. Discuss differences of opinion regarding germinal ideas, titles, forms, settings, characters, plots, and dialogue.

8. Figure out ways of arriving at creative solutions to individual and group writing and personality problems.

9. Ask questions about ideas or procedures that are unclear before making final decisions.

10. Come to a consensus over various student ideas by communicating and negotiating.

11. Fill in character analysis worksheet with a character that fits the context of the play.

12. Orally share the internal, external, and symbolic aspects of the character with peers while they listen and take notes on the scenario worksheets in the playwriting workbooks.

13. Record title, form, setting, character, and plot ideas on scenario worksheets in playwriting workbooks.

14. Create dialogue for one scene from the play, in a group of 3 to 5 people, with all of the group members sharing the writing responsibilities.

15. Orally read through first play draft, as a group, and write transitions, correct illogical dialogue, actions, spelling, grammatical and other script errors.

16. Hand in character, scenario, and dialogue assignments by preset deadlines in order to keep group project functioning.

17. Note how character internal and external aspects created by class members, as well as play circumstances, reflect on lives and problems of class.

EVALUATION

1. Given a quiz over key playwriting concepts and vocabulary, the students will spell and define them with at least a score of 70%.

2. Notebooks are handed in weekly and checked for content, organization, and writing abilities.

3. Individual one-act germinal ideas are thought up and listed on germinal idea section of playwriting workbook.

4. Brainstormed ideas are written in workbooks, verbally shared with class, and recorded as a group.

5. Germinal ideas are talked about in terms of feasibility, group interest, relevance to students' lives, and potential audience.

6. Ideas are verbally categorized according to types and criteria under the germinal idea section in the workbook; the results are recorded in playwriting workbooks.

7. Questions are asked, explanations and/or examples are given explaining concepts or how ideas might work and constructive comments are made.

8. Oral discrimination is made between ideas that fit the class' overall playwriting concept, and those that don't.

9. Oral discussion, negotiation, and consensus over all individuals' ideas are arrived at by the entire group's participation.

10. Character analysis and scenarios are filled in with at least 70% accuracy.

11. Class members constructively work with new ideas, and group decisions without dwelling on past ideas or harboring ill feelings.

12. Small groups write scenes of dialogue which fit into the agreed play outline, express characters, carry action forward, and reveal the playwrights' intended thoughts.

13. Writing work within groups is delegated fairly and group stays on task with a minimum of irrelevant comments.

14. Differences of opinion are settled between students within groups with teacher intervention or guidance only if necessary.

15. First draft of the script is given an oral read through with students reading their parts and correctly writing in new lines, transitions, spelling, punctuation, and other grammatical corrections.

16. Given a final unit evaluation, students will identify how they feel about content, process, interest level and other curriculum items with honesty.

HOW TO USE THIS UNIT

The playwriting unit which follows is written as an instructional workbook. You may copy the booklet section off for your students and let them keep the booklet in their notebooks for current and future references or you may teach playwriting using only the vocabulary list, character analysis and scenario forms if you like. The workbook is set up for between 15 and 25 students so you may have to make adjustments, say in how many people write scenes or you may have to make extra copies of the part of the scenario where students take notes on each other's characters, based on your group size. You can also run off the plays I've offered as examples and let each student keep their own or you can run off a class set and use them over for each new group of students you work with. There are several references in the workbook about these plays, so you will need to have them as references no matter which route you choose to go. You are also welcome to perform either of the plays included, free of royalties, as my students and I offer them to the public with no charge.

Throughout the writing process, improvisation activities such as those found in Viola Spolin's *Improvisation for the Theatre* can be quite useful. The sections in the process where these can be most helpful will be in determining or improving your characters (Spolin's **who** games), your setting (Spolin's **where** games), and in creating realistic dialogue. Also if you have the time or if you run into a writing snag, it's great to be able to stop writing and get students physically involved in experimenting with settings, characters or dialogue. Spolin also has exercises dealing with time, weather, conflict and other areas important to the development of a play.

I'd also like to add, that if you can steer kids away from the world of t.v., videos, internet and movies long enough to write a play, you may find yourself dealing with content that is real to students' lives. It may address issues and characters students confront daily. This is not to say they should merely imitate life, but go on to heighten what they experience in order to make it strong drama. In addition, you may be able to integrate other subjects such as history (maybe even team teach with a social science teacher) into your playwriting process (see integrated education model at the end of this section). One play included in this book deals with a historic time period and both plays included deal with with issues real to teenagers. They may not win Pulitzer Prizes, but they are adolescent expressions worthy of sharing with others.

We've enjoyed producing our plays for others by inviting families, students and their teachers to join us, with a sack lunch, and see noontime "peer plays". You could also possibly have several plays go up on one night and have an evening of one-acts. If you do go into production, you may find many of Spolin's games are also helpful throughout the rehearsal process. Games such as **give and take focus**, **stage picture**, **activity**, and **conversation with involvement** are excellent rehearsal aids. Improvisation adds life, energy, and spontaneity to your production and in the advent of a missed line or absent character, the improvisation skill can keep your production going. Whether your class writes a play, enters it into one of the numerous state or national playwriting contests, or produces it, I hope you and your group enjoy participating in the writing process. Playwriting has been going on for thousands of years and it's my hope that this book, in some small way, will help young people get enthused about the process and insure the future of this time-tested art form.

SKILL ORIENTED INTEGRATED EDUCATION MODEL
LANGUAGE ARTS--THEATRE ARTS--SOCIAL SCIENCE

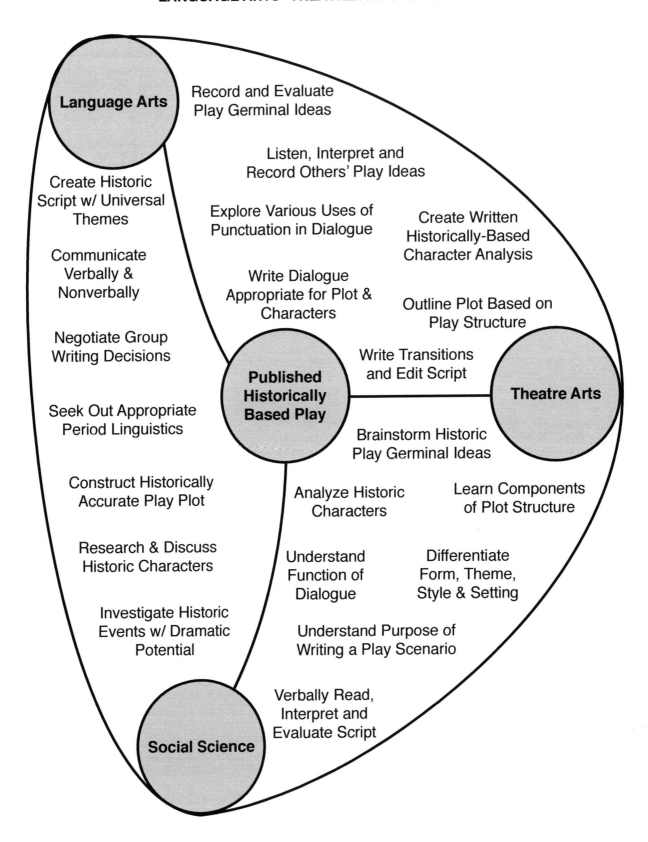

Language Arts

Record and Evaluate Play Germinal Ideas

Listen, Interpret and Record Others' Play Ideas

Create Historic Script w/ Universal Themes

Explore Various Uses of Punctuation in Dialogue

Create Written Historically-Based Character Analysis

Communicate Verbally & Nonverbally

Write Dialogue Appropriate for Plot & Characters

Outline Plot Based on Play Structure

Negotiate Group Writing Decisions

Published Historically Based Play

Write Transitions and Edit Script

Theatre Arts

Seek Out Appropriate Period Linguistics

Brainstorm Historic Play Germinal Ideas

Construct Historically Accurate Play Plot

Analyze Historic Characters

Learn Components of Plot Structure

Research & Discuss Historic Characters

Understand Function of Dialogue

Differentiate Form, Theme, Style & Setting

Investigate Historic Events w/ Dramatic Potential

Understand Purpose of Writing a Play Scenario

Verbally Read, Interpret and Evaluate Script

Social Science

PART TWO
PLAYWRITING UNIT WORKBOOK

PLAYWRITING UNIT WORKBOOK

During the next 2-3 weeks your class will be writing a one-act play together. You will begin by coming up with a germinal idea, move on to finding a form for this idea, create a working title, setting, cast of characters, and plot. Later you'll write dialogue, action, and transitions for various scenes and then join the scenes together into one unified act through the process of editing.

PLAYWRITING VOCABULARY

- playwriting - the act of composing a theatrical script on paper

- playwright - a person who writes plays; a dramatist

- brainstorming - freely letting ideas over a given subject pop into your head within a given time period without criticizing

- germinal idea - the thought that captures the earliest stages of development and is the basis for the formulation of a play

- scenario - the written outline of a play's title, format, setting, characters, and plot

- working title - the temporary heading or name given to a play-in-progress which captures the germinal idea

- format - the shape or general make-up of a play (ie. drama, comedy, fantasy...)

- drama - a serious-natured play with central character(s) trying to overcome obstacles

- tragedy - a serious form of drama with the central character(s) suffering more than they deserve while trying to overcome powerful obstacle and usually dying in the process

- melodrama - a play with exaggerated themes of seriousness arising from the threat of a bad character to a good one and with the good character overcoming all obstacles

- comedy - a humorous form of drama which is usually light-hearted in nature and upholds normal situations and character by poking fun at abnormal ones; central characters overcome an entangled mesh of obstacles

- fantasy - a serious or humorous play form which usually combines mortal and non-mortal characters who overcome obstacles in the land of make-believe

- setting - the place, time, and circumstances in which a play unfolds

- character analysis - the planning or understanding of the internal, external, and symbolic aspects of a role, usually outlined in written form

- plot - the structured action of a play including the exposition, where characters and situations are introduced; the complications, where problems and obstacles arise; the climax, where all conflicts come to a peak; and the resolution, where all the problems unravel or at least come to a resting place

- dialogue - the written words or conversations in a script which a character uses to express his/her feelings, beliefs, motivations, and other personality aspects

- editing - the process of reading, correcting, rearranging, cutting, and rewriting a play-in-progress in order to form a correct and unified publication

BRAINSTORMING THE GERMINAL IDEA

A germinal idea is the basis for the formulation of a play. The word germinal means "in the earliest stages of development; productive of new ideas..."It parallels the word 'germinate', meaning "sprout, bud, produce." Think of the germinal idea as a seed ready to grow. It has all the potential for a fully developed play idea condensed into a word or two.

A germinal idea has to have three requirements to be of use to a playwright. 1)It must command an interest in the writer(s). 2)It must have potential for dramatic stage production. 3)It must be capable of intensifying life and contacting the audience. Remember also, you are not going to be writing a film, television series, commercial, or video. You are writing a play to be done on one setting on a stage, with anywhere from 15-25 characters (depending on how many people are in your class), which takes place over a short period of time (20-30 minutes).

Five types of germinal ideas follow:

1) based on people and their behavior 2) based on a place 3) based on an event 4) based on a thought 5) based on historic or other information.

Before you begin the following activity make sure you understand the above criteria and types of germinal ideas. Ask your questions or for examples, if you are not clear on any information covered so far. Now, on the lines below, individually list as many germinal ideas as you can in the next 3 minutes; we'll share them as a group later.

One-act Germinal Ideas Brainstorming_____

_____

_____

_____

_____

_____

_____

_____

_____

_____

_____

_____

_____

It's time to share your ideas with the rest of the class. Your teacher or another class member will take everyone's ideas and put them on the board, one at a time, until everyone is out of ideas. Remember <u>not</u> to evaluate ideas yet. Look at the definition of 'brainstorming' under vocabulary if you're not sure what it means.

After all the ideas are recorded you start evaluating the class' ideas based on the criteria at the beginning of this section. Label whether the idea meets the first three criteria and what type of idea it is (ie. based on a thought, event, etc.). Don't be afraid to combine, rearrange, or separate ideas. After you've sorted through all of these germinal ideas you'll need to decide on your top three choices as a class. Discuss the possibilities for these top three ideas in more detail. Try to come to a consensus on which idea you want to go with by negotiating rather than voting. Once you've reached a decision, write the class' decision on the next line.

Germinal Idea_____

DEVELOPING THE SCENARIO

You're ready to write your scenario now, but make sure you've let go of all the other ideas you've talked about for play possibilities and commit to the one the class has chosen.

The scenario is an outline to organize notes, thoughts, and other collected materials the playwright has accumulated. At this stage the writer(s) must struggle with shaping these materials into the best form to express what s/he is after. It is the step that comes before writing the play's dialogue and action and is important in creating a well made play. The scenario format was first used by wandering groups of performers in Europe after theatre was banned by the churches after the fall of the Roman Empire. These performers would write up an outline of what they were to perform each day and would improvise, or make up the play's dialogue as they went along. This art form was called Commedia dell'Arte and all that the performers knew before they went on stage was the show's title, setting, form, cast of characters, and plot outline. These are also the components you need to know before writing out a play in scripted form.

You have already brainstormed over a germinal idea. Now you need to consider what working title best fits your idea. The working title tells what your play is about in a nut-shell. Later you may want to change the title to something fancier or more artistic, but for now, each of you by yourself, brainstorm three ideas for a title in the next minute and write these ideas down in the spaces below

Working Titles_____

_____

_____

Share your ideas with your class. Your teacher will write them on the board. Think about the value of each title, discuss it with your class, come to a consensus on one, and write it on the space labeled 'working title' on **The Scenario Sheet** (located near end of workbook).

Format refers to form or whether your play is a tragedy, drama, melodrama, comedy, or fantasy. It's helpful for you read examples of these formats before you choose a form for your play. Two plays appear at the back of this book. These plays were written by 7th and 8th graders who followed this unit plan. Definitions for these forms appear under the vocabulary section at the beginning of this workbook.

Your class should decide whether your germinal idea best fits the category of tragedy, drama, melodrama, comedy, or fantasy. Discuss what form you think would best organize your thoughts and express what meaning you want to communicate to your intended audience. Make a choice as a group and then go with the class' decision. Write your result on the line labeled 'format' on **The Scenario Sheet**.

Setting refers to the time and place where a play unfolds. For a one-act you want one setting. Your setting should reflect a place that is right for your idea. Look at how the setting selected for each of the plays included with this book fit the idea behind the show. Take a couple of minutes to think of a good place and time to reflect the mood, meaning, and action you have in mind. Write down a couple of ideas in the next few minutes on the lines below. Jot down a reason for your choice of time and place next to the idea.

Setting_____

_____

Time Period_____

_____

Once more, share your ideas, record them on the board, evaluate the possibilities, come to an agreement with your class and record it under the line marked 'setting' on **The Scenario Sheet**.

The next step in writing a scenario is to come up with a cast of characters. Each class member will be creating their own, but before you can go to work on your character, you all must talk about what general types of characters you think would best fit your play idea. List five character types on the lines below and note how they would fit the germinal idea, format, and setting you've established. Remember, to have a play you'll need central or main characters, opposing characters or those against the central character, and contributing characters or those that support either the central or opposing types. There are places provided to note each character type.

Central Characters_____

_____

Support to Central Characters_____

_____

Opposing Characters_____

_____

Support to Opposing Characters_____

_____

Now, as a group, list at least 30 choices on the board and discuss which ones fit your play idea best. Circle the ones you think will make your play most comic or dramatic. Make sure you have all three kinds of characters or your play won't have conflict. Divvy up the characters until everyone has a character assignment and you have a balance of different character types. Then move onto having each actor fill out an 'Analyzing Your Character' form for their specific character.

The 'Analyzing Your Character' form starts by asking you to create a name for your character. The name should tell something about the time period and personality of your character. You may end up coming up with the name of the character after you finish fleshing out their other character aspects. In other words, just because it's first on the form doesn't have to mean that's where you have to begin. If you need more ideas you can look at the two plays from Part 3 of this book.

When you get to the <u>background</u>, of your character form, you should decide what their family was like, important things that happened to them as they grew up and basically everything that has made them who they are as an individual. Perhaps they fell into a well as a child and now they are afraid of water. Or their mother could have read super hard books out loud to them, before they were even born, and now they are a little genius. Perhaps they came from a military family and everything has to be 'done by the book' and the person also likes to give a lot of orders.

The <u>mental</u> section investigates how they learn. For instance, do they learn by making lots of mistakes, by hands on experiences or just by watching? There are many ways to take in the world, so seek out how they do it. <u>Spiritual</u> looks at what they look towards for guidance and in whom or what they have faith. They could worship God or something else, depending on what is important to them and how they were raised. A character whose family is very wealthy, may hold money in high regard or a chef may look to food for answers. You decide.

The emotional aspect checks out how their feelings operate most of the time. They could be quick to temper, overly calm, or secretly jealous of others. They might be happy on the outside, but sad deep down inside. It's important to explore. Social aspects will delve into whether your character is a loner, social butterfly, natural leader or even a follower. It also looks at where they fit into the world. If they spent lots of time in the woods and with nature, maybe they don't like T.V.'s, computers, phones or anything that is electronic.

The motive is the most important area to figure out. It's closely tied to the background area. An example might be that someone from a large family, where the parents were gone a lot, might seek out a lot of attention and may act out to get it. Another example could be a person who moved several times a year, as a young child, might feel like an outsider, insecure or like they have no friends. A child of a family of clowns might be one themselves or they might go to the opposite extreme and be very serious.

The external aspects should directly relate to the internals. For instance, if you have someone who is moody and has dark thoughts, maybe they dress in black. Someone who feels passed over and neglected, might have hunched over posture.A character who is easily excited might have jumpy movements. This also applies to symbolic traits. A character that is extremely happy might have a sunflower as their plant, yellow for their color, a canary for their animal and a lightbulb for their design. Someone who is all wound up may have a rabbit for an animal, an ivy for their plant, lime green for their color and a spring for a design.

This part of writing a play can be a lot of fun as well as quite interesting. So... go ahead and start filling in this character analysis, (on the next page) putting a lot of thought and creativity into it and making sure all of the parts of the role fit together into one unified person.

ANALYZING YOUR CHARACTER

Character's Name_____

Internal Aspects (What's inside the character, makes him tick?)

Background (What are important events in his her life's story?)

_____

_____

_____(use back if necessary)

Mental (How smart is s/he and how does s/he learn?)_____

_____

Spiritual (What are his/her beliefs, values, and life ideas?)_____

_____

Emotional (How does your character feel most of the time?)_____

_____

Social (How does s/he get along with others and why?)_____

_____

Motives (What drives him/her to act or be the way s/he is?)_____

_____

_____

External (What the audience sees as result of internal aspects)

Posture (How does s/he stand?)_____

Movements (How does s/he move?)_____

Age (How old is s/he?)_____

Dress (Describe typical outfit)_____

Voice (Describe range and quality)_____

Habits (Repetitive actions)_____

Symbolic (Object or idea representing your character's essence)

Name his/her plant_____animal_____

color_____ draw pattern or design in the box (representing inner forces)

_____
| |
| |
| |
| |
| |
|_____|

Turn to the section of **The Scenario Sheet** marked 'cast of characters and descriptions'. The next step in developing your play is to have each person in your class go up before everyone else and slowly, clearly, and loudly share all the elements of his/her character with everyone else. The class will take brief notes on each person's character, next to each space. On the first line write your classmate's name; on the second put his/her character's name. Under 'I' put his/her character's internals, under 'E' put his/her externals, and under 'S' put symbolic. Each person should be given 3-5 minutes to share in order to get through this in 2 class periods. Remember, after the character descriptions and plot outline is done you'll be breaking into groups and writing lines for all the different characters in your play; so listen, take careful notes, and ask questions about people's characters when they're finished (if some aspect was not clear).

The final step in writing a scenario is the plot or scene outline. If you look at the definition of 'plot' and 'form' (under vocabulary list), you'll see that there are four basic parts to a one-act and each form has a different plot type. Take a couple of minutes to study this information and ask your instructor to clear up any problems you have understanding it.

Now you're ready for your final brainstorming session. You're looking for action that fits all elements of your developing play from your title to your characters. Each of you, on your own, list one or two ideas for exposition, complications, climax, and resolution. You have five minutes to write down your plot ideas.

Brainstorming Plot Ideas

Exposition_____

_____

Complications_____

_____

Climax_____

_____

Resolution_____

_____

It's time to share your ideas with the group. Everyone should first share their exposition ideas; the teacher or a class member can write all these ideas under 'exposition' on the board. Then do the same for complications, climax and resolution. Discuss which ideas could work together to make an exciting story. Decide on favorites and then turn to the section of **The Scenario Sheet** marked 'plot outline'.

On the outline section, of the scenario sheet, you'll see scenes I-4. Scene 1 is exposition, scene 2 complications, scene 3 is climax and scene 4 is the resolution. Put the ideas from each category on the board in the best order and then record them under the appropriate scenes on **The Scenario Sheet**. Generally speaking, all your characters, the main action of the play, and the first complication should be introduced somehow in the first scene. The next two scenes thicken the plot. Things get more and more complicated. The central character tries to solve the problems as they arise and the opposing character makes things worse. When the action can go no further, because everything is so complicated, you've reached the climax.During the last scene all the problems must quickly resolve and the play must come to an end or conclusion.

THE SCENARIO SHEET

Working Title_____

Format_____

Setting_____

Cast of Characters and Descriptions

(**I**= Internal Traits   **E**= External Traits   **S**= Symbolic Character Qualities)

_____I_____
(student's name)

_____I_____
(character name)

                       I_____

                       E_____

                       S_____

_____I_____

_____I_____

I_____

E_____

S_____

_____I_____

_____I_____

I_____

E_____

S_____

_____ I _____

_____ I _____

I _____

E _____

S _____

_____ I _____

_____ I _____

I _____

E _____

S _____

_____I_____

_____I_____

I_____

E_____

S_____

_____I_____

_____I_____

I_____

E_____

S_____

_____I_____

_____I_____

                I_____

                E_____

                S_____

_____I_____

_____I_____

                I_____

                E_____

                S_____

_____I_____

_____I_____

               I_____

               E_____

               S_____

_____I_____

_____I_____

               I_____

               E_____

               S_____

I_____I_____

I_____I_____

I_____

E_____

S_____

I_____I_____

I_____I_____

I_____

E_____

S_____

_____I_____

_____I_____

I_____

E_____

S_____

_____I_____

_____I_____

I_____

E_____

S_____

Plot Outline

Scene 1 (Exposition)_____

_____

_____

_____

_____

_____

_____

_____

_____

_____

_____

Scene 2 (Complications)_____

_____

_____

_____

_____

_____

_____

_____

_____

_____

_____

Scene 3 (Climax)_____

Scene 4 (Resolution)

WRITING AND EDITING THE DIALOGUE AND ACTION

Dialogue, in drama, consists of the written words or conversation in a script which a character uses to express his/her thoughts. Playwrights have to use words to express all aspects of their characters' personalities. Words are more than mere conveyors of meaning; they have artistic qualities like rhythm, shape, movement, texture, color, level, pitch, and tone. To a playwright words are the material used to build an expressive play. As you begin to choose words, therefore, select them carefully. Make sure they're the right word for the right moment. Come up with words that seem natural coming from the mouths of your characters. After all, not all people react to surprise with the same verbal expressions. Everyone has his/her pet expressions and so will your characters. Take a couple of minutes to think up and write a line of dialogue for your character in response to each of the following situations.

S/he just opens a gift and it's something s/he has really wanted for a long time.

_____

_____

S/he has just had his/her foot stepped on._____

_____

S/he can't figure out how to solve a puzzle of some sort._____

_____

Take a few minutes as a class to share these character reactions with each other. Let each other know which expressions seem to fit characters best and which seem off target. Listen to conversations. Become aware of the way people put together conversations in small and large groups. Not all lines of dialogue need to be complete sentences or merely spoken by one person. Punctuation can be used to give dialogue its timing and to show incomplete or cut off sentences. A sentence of exclamation can be just a word followed by an exclamation point. A broken sentence can just be a couple of words followed by a dash. An elliptical sentence can have a series of thoughts connected by ellipses.... See if you can find an example of an exclamatory, broken, or elliptical sentence from the plays in the back of this booklet. Write some examples on the board. Here are three examples to get you started.

Exclamatory Dialogue Example:

WOMAN

Help! (Flailing her arms)

Broken Dialogue Example:

MAN

(With alarm) What do you-

Elliptical Dialogue Example:

WOMAN

I'm... ack... choking...

These kinds of sentences can be mixed with complete grammatically correct sentences, of course. You need all kinds of sentences, for variety, in writing lines of dialogue. Each character you write for will have his/her own kind of sentence that fits him/her. Somebody who is impatient may cut everyone off all the time. Someone who has gone to all the best schools may only speak in perfectly punctuated English. Also, notice from the above examples and from the plays accompanying this, that play dialogue is not surrounded by quotation marks. Usually the character's name appears in the left margin, followed by a colon or dash, and then the words of dialogue. The character name can also appear, centered, right above the line of dialogue. Parentheses enclose all stage and acting directions and can appear anywhere in a line of dialogue; if well placed they can break up a thought like punctuation.

You've finally reached the point where you can begin to write your play in script form. Your teacher will break you up into 4 groups; one group will write each scene from your play. It helps if people with different writing abilities are in each group. It also helps if the groups sit numerically ordered so if scene 1 wants to know how scene 2 is going to start their scene they're right next each other and can discuss problems and solutions that come up both within the small group assigned and between the groups. Each person in the group should get a chance to write at least a half of page of dialogue while the others are helping them think up action and dialogue as they write. Try and make sure every character has at least one line of dialogue per scene if possible. Your finished scene should be 5 pages double spaced or 2-3 single spaced if your total play is going to run 20-30 minutes.

A common mistake among beginning playwrights is to rush through what you outlined on the plot section of **The Scenario Sheet**. Remember the audience wants a chance to get to know who the characters are, what is going on, and what thoughts or meanings your play contains. Take enough time to develop a scene that has plenty of dramatic action built in, and in which all the characters are reacting and interrelating. Anytime someone in your cast of characters says or does something, consider how it would affect everyone else in the play. Would they step back, chime in with a comment, cut the other character off or simply make a facial expression? You'll have three class meetings to write your scenes. Then a group member can type up the scene for extra-credit, and get it into the teacher so s/he can get enough copies made so you can read through and edit your script.

Once everyone has a first draft of the whole script you'll start the final step in playwriting known as redrafting or editing. Sit in a circle having your script and a pencil ready. Each person reads their own part aloud and the teacher can read the stage directions. The first time you read through the script make notes about lines you think need changing, places in the script that seem to have something missing, or anything else that seems to need work. You'll probably have to abbreviate to have time to write during the course of the reading.

Before starting to read through the script again try and locate major problems and make a list of them on the board. Major problems would be large sections of important action that were left out or if a character ended up with no lines. Discuss possible solutions. You might have to write some short scenes to insert where there are gaps in the script. You could also write in lines for missing characters during your second edit.

Once you've solved major problems go back and read through the script as a group again. Correct inappropriate lines, spelling, punctuation, and add in lines or take them out where necessary. Write in transitions from scene to scene if they're missing or weak. Check the overall flow of the play. Does the overall action make sense? Are you communicating the germinal idea you had in mind? Does your character seem to work in every scene? This is your last chance to polish up your script before students volunteer to type up scenes, get them into the teacher, so the second draft can be run off and compiled. Once this is done you'll have a play your whole class can act out if you like; if you do you'll probably keep improving your script as you go.

EVALUATION

Make sure you understand the vocabulary list at the front of this unit. You are responsible for spelling and defining the words on the list. You should also be able to give an example that shows you understand the term.Study the list with a partner. Verbally quiz each other. Tomorrow your teacher will give you a vocabulary test. It may be fill in the blank or something of their own design.

When you're through with the play and test please fill out the unit evaluation form on the next page. This way your teacher will know what to improve in this unit and how you liked it.

COURSE EVALUATION FORM

Please rate each of the following statements by circling the numbers below:

1 = extremely   2 = pretty good   3 = okay   4 = not very   5 = not at all

1. Writing a one-act play was interesting.   1 2 3 4 5

2. Having your own booklet and scenario was good.   1 2 3 4 5

3. Studying vocabulary helped me with playwriting.   1 2 3 4 5

4. This playwriting unit was challenging.   1 2 3 4 5

5. Brainstorming gets everyone involved in creating.   1 2 3 4 5

6. Working in different sized groups was fun.   1 2 3 4 5

7. Having to go along with group decisions was hard.   1 2 3 4 5

8. My playwriting skills improved during this project.   1 2 3 4 5

9. Making and sticking to time deadlines is important.   1 2 3 4 5

10. I learned new things about myself and others.   1 2 3 4 5

(Hand this entire booklet into your teacher so s/he can give you useful suggestions on how to improve your writing skills. You will get to keep the booklet later.)

PART THREE
THE PLAYS

THE HANG OUT

A Drama in One Act

This play was written by the third rotation middle school Exploratory Drama class at U.N.C.'s Lab School in the spring of 1988 and used by permission of student playwrights.

Cast of Characters:

Kandice -good samaritan type --waitress at The Hang Out

Peter - fighter from a broken home --cook at The Hang Out

Justin - star athlete, fights to prove himself

Margie - shy athlete from well-to-do family

Brittany - conceited and popular leader-of-the-clique type

Audrey - rich and catty "in-clique" type

Angie - social gossip who thereafter feels guilty

Alley - popular but sometimes insecure socialite

Joe - low-achieving fighter and ladies' man

Sam - high-achiever following the crowd and trying to fit in

Misty - friendly, out-going and well-to-do peer counselor

Andica - sensible and steadfast do-gooder type

Chris - defensive loner looking for a place to fit in

Setting

This play takes place in the after school Hang Out which has a snack-bar with several stools on the stage right side and three tables with four chairs at each on the center and stage left side. There is a door to the cafe up center, door to the kitchen center right and door to the restrooms center stage left. The lights should be brought up to half at the start of the scene and then a follow spot can be used to highlight conversation and focus, by moving from table to table as needed. Actors may need to quietly improvise dialogue when the focus is not on them.

SCENE 1

(Kandace unlocks the Hang Out and hums her favorite tune while she straightens up tables and turns on the t.v. located at the bar. Peter enters.)

PETER

Hey, toots, how's it going? (sits on bar and puts his feet up on a stool)

KANDACE

Stop calling me "toots" (pulls stool out from under his legs) and it's going okay. We have lots of work to do, Peter, so we'd better get going. (hands him dish cloth)

PETER

(draping cloth around her neck) I don't want to work, toots.

KANDACE

(snaps him with the towel) For the last time, stop calling me "toots" and get to work.

PETER

(jumping up) Okay, toots, (she glares at him) just kidding, Kandace. I'll go get the mop and you go get the burgers going. (they exit for a moment)

KANDACE

(wiping up tables as Peter enters with a mop)So, what are you doing tonight?

PETER

I'm gonna fight--

KANDACE

(cutting him off) What?! I thought you told me you weren't going to fight anymore?

PETER

Well--

KANDACE

So, who are you going to roll around on the ground with this time?

PETER

(playfully) Well not with you, that's for sure.

KANDACE

(giving him a light smack with her waitress pad)
Peter... well with who then?

PETER

Justin Hawk.

KANDACE

The captain of the basketball team?

PETER

You got it and here he comes ri-i-ight now with
his "protector" Margie.

(Margie and Justin enter talking about the bad refereeing at the game and sit at the
stool as Kandace shuffles Peter off trying to avoid any fighting.)

KANDACE

Peter, remember, you need this job so don't
you lay a finger on him.

(Peter pushes Justin out of his way with one finger as he passes the bar on his
way into the kitchen)

JUSTIN

(jumping up from his stool and ready to fight)
What's that, your hardest punch?

PETER

You'll find out later.

MARGIE

(pulling Justin away from Peter) Come on
guys, let it rest.

KANDACE

(pulling Peter toward kitchen) Yah, guys--

PETER

(still ready to fight) After work.

JUSTIN

Yah! Later!

(As the near fight cools down, Brittany and Audrey walk in talking about Kandace.)

BRITTANY

Oh, did you hear about Kandace? I heard she had to get this job because her parents are going down. (they head for the table furthest stage right)

AUDREY

Yah. I heard that her dad was having an affair with his secretary at work and his wife found out!

BRITTANY

Sh-h-h, here she comes. (they put on false smiles as Kandace walks over with her pencil and pad)

KANDACE

Hey guys, what do you want?

BRITTANY

Well, I'll have a sundae and make sure that's without "nuts." (she makes a sign to Audrey likes it's Kandace who's nuts.)

AUDREY

(giggles coyly) I'll have a DIET Coke because I have to watch my figure.

KANDACE

(talking under her breath as she heads up to the bar to make the sundae) Yah, you would have to watch your weight.

AUDREY

(turns and glares at Kandace) What was that?

KANDACE

(loudly) Nothin' honey. (a cereal reference)

PETER

(popping his head out from the kitchen) Who wants cereal at this time of day?

KANDACE

Never mind. (places order with Peter)

(Peter and Kandace talk quietly as do Margie and Justin and Brittany and Audrey as the focus shifts to Angie and Alley who enter having a serious conversation about Angie's home life.)

ANGIE

Hi, Kandace. (Kandace waves as Angie grabs
Alley's arm and they head to the stage left
table) Alley, do you promise not to tell my
secret to anyone?

ALLEY

(with false conviction) Sure, Angie... (they sit
and notice Audrey and Brittany)

ANGIE

Let's go sit with Brittany and Audrey, they
always have good gossip.

(The focus quickly jumps back to Brittany and Audrey as Angie and Alley get up
and cross over to their table.)

BRITTANY

Well, anyway, back to Kandace... I didn't know
Kandace's dad was having an affair, who told
you this?

AUDREY

Sh-h-h, here comes Angie, she'll probably go
and tell Kandace. (Angie has overheard the
gossip already, though, but pretends not to
have.)

ANGIE

Hi, guys.

BRITTANY AND AUDREY

(smiling falsely) Hi.

ANGIE

(looking over at Kandace and then back) Ah...
I'll be right back, okay? (getting up and heading
toward restrooms)

ALLEY

What do you want and I'll order for you?

ANGIE

I'll have a Coke.

(She motions for Kandace to meet her in the restroom as Joe and Sam enter
talking about their fathers.)

                            SAM
Last night my dad hit me because I got a "B" in
trig.

                            JOE
So, if my dad hits me, I hit him back.

                            SAM
Right, Joe.

                            JOE
I do. Hey, there's Brit. (he winks at her and she
snubs his attentions)

                            SAM
What's up?

                            JOE
You got me...

(Joe and Sam sit at the downstage left table as Misti and Andica enter with Chris,
who is a first time customer of the Hang Out, attracts looks and whispers.)

                          MISTI
(beaming) Hi, guys!

                        KANDACE
(entering from the bathroom with Angie
following her) Hi, Misti.

                          MISTI
You all know Chris...

                            ALL
(ad libbing) Hi.

                          CHRIS
(shyly) Hi.

(They sit down at the center table and the focus shifts to Audrey Brittany, and
Alley.)

                          AUDREY
I can't believe Misti and Andica are hanging
around with Chris.

                        BRITTANY
(snotty) I know.

ALLEY

(carefully) He's not so bad once you get to know him.

BRITTANY

(looking at Alley strangely) What's there to know?

ANGIE

(returning to the table) Alley, I saw Kandace in the restroom and told her to order us a couple of Cokes, okay?

ALLEY

(troubled) Sure.

KANDACE

(walking up with a tray) Here is your sundae, Brittany. Here is your Diet Coke, Audrey. And here are your Cokes, Angie and Alley.

ALL
(AD LIBBING) THANKS.
MARGIE

(calling out) Kandi, will you get me a Coke please?

KANDACE

(walking to the snack bar to make sure Margie and Justin have everything they need) Sure. Anything else?

(The focus shifts back to Misti, Chris, and Andica)

CHRIS

So, this is where all of you hang out after school. (looks around evaluating his surroundings)

MISTI

(enthusiastically) Well... what do you think?

CHRIS

I don't know yet.

ANDICA

Well, wait 'til you taste the food.

Scene 2

(Joe gets up and crosses to Brittany. She gets up as he nears, looks at him coldly, and goes to the snack bar to flirt with Peter. Joe is floored and starts asking the girls at Brittany's table what's going on as Brittany and Peter take focus.)

BRITTANY
(pulling Peter aside) Hi Peter. How are you?

PETER
(wondering) Fine, Brittany.

BRITTANY
(looking back at Joe) So what are you doing tonight?

PETER
Nothing much... (smiles knowingly at Justin, who taps his hand with his fist) So, aren't you still going out with Joe?

BRITTANY
(looking at Joe smugly as she gets closer to Peter) Well, I don't know if he's gotten the picture yet, but I'm really getting sick of him!

PETER
What 'da-ya' mean, Brit?

BRITTANY
(sighs) What I mean is I'm just sick of his fighting.

PETER
(guilty) Oh... you don't like guys who fight, huh?

BRITTANY
Not really.

PETER
(changing the subject) Well, I've gotta cook up an order now. I'll be talking with ya'.

(Peter slips away. Brittany walks to her table, clears her throat to get Joe to get up and leave, which he does. The focus goes with him as he goes and talks with Sam who has been taking everything in that's been going on around him.)

SAM
So what's the story?

JOE

I don't know, she won't talk to me.

KANDACE

(walking up to take their order) Are you ready?

JOE

(looking over at the girls) I'm always ready.

KANDACE

(bops Joe on the head with her pad) Joe...!

JOE

Just kidding! I'll have a quarter pound hamburger and make that rare, with fries and a Mountain Dew.

SAM

Joe, did you bring any money?

JOE

(hitting himself on the head with his palm) Dude, I forgot!

SAM

Way to go.

KANDACE

(wondering) Well...?

SAM

(sighing) I've got some money, Joe.

JOE

Thanks, man, I owe you one. (gives Sam a "high five")

(As Kandace gets the rest of the guys' order, the focus switches back to the girls' table.)

ANGIE

Joe is such a jerk.

ALLEY

I know what you mean.

BRITTANY

Yah, and he always sponges off of Sam. I don't know why he even hangs out with him.

AUDREY

He never has any money because his dad
blows all their money at the bar.

JOE

(overhears Audrey and stands up yelling)
What, are you writing a book on my life or
something?

AUDREY

(sarcastically) There's nothing to write, Joe.

BRITTANY

(disgusted) Cool it you guys! (she starts to walk
away past Joe's table and he grabs her arm
and swings her around)

JOE

So... Brittany, what ya' doin' tonight?

BRITTANY

(shaking his hand off of her arm) Nothing with
you, Joe.

(She walks away to talk to Peter as Joe stands shocked. Chris has been listening
and getting angry with Brittany; Misti and Andica are trying to calm him down in the
background.)

SAM

Joe.

JOE

What?

SAM

Sit down.

JOE

Yah, right.

SAM

Aren't you still going out with Brittany?

JOE

I... don't know...

(Brittany and Peter take focus and Chris starts over towards them hesitantly.)

BRITTANY

I think he got the picture.

PETER

Yah, I think so too.

CHRIS

(awkwardly) Um... Brittany?

BRITTANY

(annoyed) What do you want, Chris?

CHRIS

I overheard you talking with Joe and I think you
were a little hard--

BRITTANY

(loud and sarcastic) Oh, you can think?

AUDREY

(standing) And he can talk too!

(Everyone is now staring at Chris.)

BRITTANY

Let's give him a hand, everyone!

(Half the group claps while Misti and Andica are trying to get them all to stop and
Alley sits not knowing what to do.)

Scene 3

KANDACE

(yelling and standing up center) Why don't you all just leave him alone?! (it gets instantly quiet)Nobody here has anything nice to say about anybody here... especially Audrey and Brittany!

AUDREY

(mock innocence) What!?

BRITTANY

What did we do now?

KANDACE

You know what you said.

BRITTANY

(snotty) We haven't said anything to you.

KANDACE

Not to my face, but behind my back you did.

PETER

Fight! Fight!

JOE

Waste her, Brit!

BRITTANY

(sarcastic) Waste? I'm not going to waste my time on her. I have better things to do.

AUDREY

What would you expect from someone with a dad like hers.

KANDACE

(seething) You leave my father out of this!

AUDREY

So, it's true...

(Audrey and Brittany have slowly been converging on Kandace and they get into a further tussle. Angie looks embarrassed and goes out for a moment while Andica and Misti try to break up the argument. Justin and Margie get up from the bar which is getting crowded out by the group of girls fighting. They start bouncing a basketball and making baskets in the trash can on the down right side of the bar. Peter starts over towards them)

                    JUSTIN
        They fight about everything.

                    MARGIE
        You see how stupid fighting is, Justin? (makes
        a basket) Hey, I made it. Care to have a little
        contest?

                    JUSTIN
        Why bother when you know I would beat you?

                    MARGIE
        Awe, you wish. You want to put some money on
        it?

                    JUSTIN
        Yah. How much?

                    MARGIE
        Whoever loses has to buy ice cream for the
        other for a week after school.

                    JUSTIN
        Let's go for it. (he dribbles around Alley's table)

                    ALLEY
        Don't you two ever stop?

                    JUSTIN
        No way.

(Alley goes over and talks to Chris to one side as Peter heads off Justin's shot by grabbing his arm as he's about to shoot.)

                    PETER
        If you chicks are going to play basketball, do it
        outside.

                    JUSTIN
        (leaping at Peter, but being pulled toward the
        door, right through the middle of the girl's fight,
        by Margie) I'm not a chick. If I want to play then
        I will!

                    MARGIE
        Come on Justin. Let's go outside.

(Kandace pulls Peter into the kitchen, Joe sees Brittany alone and pulls her aside.)

JOE

Why won't ya' go out with me Brit?

BRITTANY

I can't! You let me down too many times.

JOE

What are you talking about?

BRITTANY

Oh get off it, Joe... you know what I'm talking
about.

JOE

(confused) Right... Why do you have to go off
with Peter, then?

BRITTANY

Because I like him, okay?

JOE

Whatever...

BRITTANY

Joe... Fine. Don't talk to me, see if I care.

(Joe joins Sam at their table, and Brittany goes to her table, where Audrey is
sipping her drink smugly. Misti and Andica join Sam and Joe to try and counsel Joe
about his problem with Brittany. Alley and Chris take focus at Chris' table.)

ALLEY

(looking around to see if Angie is around)
Chris, there's something else I have to tell you,
but you can't tell anyone.

CHRIS

Well... I guess so... is there a problem you
have?

ALLEY

No. It's a problem one of my friends has.

CHRIS

Well... what's the problem?

ALLEY

Well you know Angie, don't you?

CHRIS

Sort of.

ALLEY

Angie's really secretive when it comes to her
parents so she surprised me when she told me
they're getting a divorce.

CHRIS

Un huh.

ALLEY

And she's really ashamed of it and she only
told me and no one else is supposed to know.

CHRIS

(puzzled) So why are you telling me then?

ALLEY

Cause I have to tell someone and get it out.
And I know you're so quiet and to yourself that
you'd never tell... I'm really upset for her.

CHRIS

(putting an arm around her shoulder, which is
what Alley was after to begin with) I know what
it's like to have a bad family life. I've never
even met my mother... and my dad... well
what's there to say... he drinks.

(Angie enters again, sees Alley with Chris and calls her as she heads back to join
Brittany and Audrey.)

ANGIE

(annoyed) Alley.

ALLEY

Well, gotta go. (reluctantly, but feeling the peer
pressure) Bye.

(Angie jumps all over Alley for being with Chris and Alley defends him; the other
two girls join in too. Kandace is getting on Peter's case for almost getting into
another fight with Justin. Chris joins Sam and Joe, who are arguing about how they
think he should have handled Brittany while Andica and Misti get up and try and
talk to one side, but can't hear from all the simultaneous fighting. When they begin
talking the others continue to fight, but it's mostly pantomimed.)

MISTI

Geez, all this fighting is really getting to me.

ANDICA

I know what you mean.

MISTI

I can't believe we come here after school to relax.

ANDICA

We need someone with a big mouth to get everyone to quiet down.

MISTI

Well don't look at me, I don't have a big mouth.

JOE

(interrupting) I do.

MISTI AND ANDICA

Great!

JOE

(standing on his table) Everyone zip it! This isn't World War III!

ANDICA

Yah! We don't come here to listen to people fight... we come here to have fun!

BRITTANY

(obnoxious)Yah, let's have some fun!

(Margie and Justin enter and see Joe on the table and everything is quiet)

MARGIE

What's going on here?

AUDREY

(twirling her finger around in the air and making fun of Andica) We're having some fun here.

SAM

We are?

Scene 4

KANDACE
(stepping out from behind where she and Peter had been arguing) So, who really won?

MARGIE AND JUSTIN
I did.

PETER
Oh yah, ya' had ta' fight a girl to win.

JUSTIN
(defensive) Oh yes.

PETER
(provoking a fight) Bring it on.

JUSTIN
(tempted) Peter, if I fight you I'll get kicked off the team, and I don't want that to happen.

PETER
(mockingly) Yah, and if I fight you I'll put you in the hospital and I don't want that to happen.

MARGIE
(sarcastically) Yah, right.

(Brittany marches up to Peter and pulls him down stage of the bar while Margie talks to Justin on the left side of the stage.)

BRITTANY
(demanding) Peter, I have to talk with you.

PETER
(annoyed) Yah?

BRITTANY
I don't want you to fight Justin.

PETER
Oh yah? Why not?!

BRITTANY
Because I like you and I don't like it when people fight like Joe does.

JOE
(overhears them and jumps up) What? You never told me that!

BRITTANY

(disgusted) Joe, I shouldn't have to tell you that. Fighting doesn't solve anything.

MARGIE

(stops talking to Justin) Yah.

JOE

Tell that to your boyfriend, not me.

PETER

(quickly) What? (to Brittany) Fighting is cool.

JOE

Yah! It gives ya' a natural high.

ANDICA

(jumping into the argument) Joe... what would a stoner like you know about a natural high?

JOE

I'm not a stoner!

ANDICA

Yah... right.

JUSTIN

(pushing through the crowd) Wait, I know what you mean, Joe. When you're fighting and people are cheering for you it makes you feel good.

KANDACE

(throwing her dishrag over her shoulder in frustration) Well, how do you think it makes the other person feel?

MISTI

(chiming in) Yah! When you fight someone you not only hurt them physically, also mentally.

AUDREY

(melodramatically) Anyone got a hankie? Those two are breaking my heart. (feigns tears)

JOE

Audrey's the only one here who's hurt mentally if ya' ask me.

BRITTANY

No, that's not true. Anyone of you guys who thinks you have to fight to feel like a man has a mental problem, whether you want to admit it or not.

ALLEY

Yah, and if a guy solves his problem another way than fighting, you call him a wimp.

ANGIE

We all know who you're talking about, Alley... Chris!

CHRIS

(fed up) What makes you say she's talking about me?

SAM

(also fed up) Yah, it could just as easily be me.

JUSTIN

(to Chris) Because you're a wimp!

PETER

(mockingly) Da... look who's talking!

BRITTANY

(yelling) You guys!!

(By now everyone is involved in the verbal fight. All the guys are gathered around Brittany arguing with her while Kandace, Misti, and Andica are at the downstage left table discussing the fighting issue as well. Audrey, Angie, and Alley are at their table arguing about Chris and take the focus after a moment at which point everyone continues arguing mostly in pantomime. Chris pulls out of the fight when he hears himself being discussed.)

ANGIE

I really don't know what's gotten into you, Alley. How come you like that nerd?

ALLEY

He's not a nerd, he's nice!

ANGIE

If you start hanging out with him, it's just a matter of time until you become a nerd just like Chris.

CHRIS

(confronting Angie) If everyone's not perfect like you and your little group, do you call them a nerd?

(Everyone has pivoted around and is looking at Angie and Chris)

ANGIE

(holding her ground, but slightly embarrassed) I'm not perfect but I'm pretty close.

CHRIS

(calculating) I suppose your family's perfect too.

ANGIE

(hesitantly) Yah...

CHRIS

Right... (looking at Alley) Well Alley told me your parents are getting a divorce.

ALLEY

(shocked) Chris!!

(Everyone is momentarily stunned.)

ANGIE

(totally taken aback and backing away from Alley and Chris) How could you, Alley? I trusted you. I thought you were my best friend?

ALLEY

(turning to Chris) And I trusted you, Chris.

SAM

(stands up on the bar and yells) Geez... why don't you all just stop and listen to yourselves! I thought we were all friends.

MISTI

(cheery in spite of the situation) We are, Sam.

SAM

If this is how friends act, then I don't need friends.

CHRIS

Me either.

ANDICA

Don't say that, Chris.

CHRIS

No, I mean it. You two drug me in here today because you said I needed to make some friends. From what I've seen I'm better off alone. (starts walking off)

ANDICA

Wait, Chris. Real friends don't act this way.

MISTI

Real friends stay with you no matter how rough things get.

SAM

She's right, Chris. Come on. I'll go with you.

(Sam and Chris exit together and Misti and Andica follow them off calling after them.)

ANDICA AND MISTI

Wait, guys.

(Alley crosses to the doorway to follow Chris, but stops to try and talk to Angie for a moment.)

ALLEY

(imploring) Angie...?

(Angie turns her back on her and Alley leaves.)

KANDACE

(looks around at everyone and throws her dishrag down) Peter, you can tell the boss that I quit.

(Kandace exits as the rest of the crowd looks around at one another awkwardly and the lights fade to black.)

(As you can see from this play, there is an overlay of social sciences and human dynamics at the core. The student writers were frustrated with all of the in-fighting that went on between various groups at school. They also wanted to address gossip, popularity, labeling, trust issues and broken families. They chose an after school setting, where all of these different characters might be able to interact, in order to bring it all to life.)

A MEDIEVAL FANTASY
A Fantasy in One Act

This play was written by the second middle school rotation of exploratory drama students at U.N.C.'s Lab School in the winter of 1987 and used by permission of student writers. The characters have two roles each. One is in the real world and the other in the fantasy.

Cast of Characters

Cindy/Maid Cynthia - Upperclass, resentful and highbrow

Kathy/Maid Katherine - Upperclass, perfectionist, social butterfly

Gabby/Maid Gabriel - Upperclass, money-oriented, gossip

Anna/Maid Anastasia - Upperclass, stylish, spoiled, and stuck up

Gwen/Queen Guinevere - Wealthy, fair, and domineering

Diane/Diana- Well - liked and worldly gypsy, full of stories

Alex/Alexia - Talkative joker and prankster

Buzz/Buzzly - Strange but oddly lovable old character

Principal Dill/Sheriff - Stern, control-oriented, and clumsy

Arty/King Arthur - Highbrow leader, social, lady's man

Lance/Sir Lancelot - Bold friend of the leader, skilled fighter

Gallager/Sir Gallahad - Gallant, bold, wealthy and aggressive

Rob/Squire Robin - Not-too-swift would-be fighter and socialite

Greg/Lord Gregory - Upperclass dropout with a secret problem

Merle/Merlin - Unusual mad-scientist-type into magic and mystics

John/Jonathan - Oddball poor boy from a broken home, loves bugs

Scott/Scotton - Wildly daring, from the wrong side of town

Dan/Delvar - Revengeful orphan, striking out at others

Setting

This play takes place in a mysterious-looking forest during present and medieval times. The background has a cutout tree drop. A rock sits down right and a tree stump center left.

Scene 1

(Principal Dill enters in a huff and yells off to a group of students who are entering carrying backpacks and other camping equipment. They are talking in their own little groups as they come on.)

MR. DILL

Hurry up children. (trips on a rock as he turns to see if they are coming) Ow!

(Cindy, Anna, Gwen, Kathy, and Gabby enter complaining about having to camp out. Diane and Alex trail on after them.)

CINDY

All these trees and things are giving me a splitting headache!

ANNA

(rolling her eyes) You always have a headache, Cindy.

KATHY

Do us a favor and take an aspirin.

GABBY

Yes, do... Cindy.

CINDY

(bowing to her mock rulers)Yes Kathy... Yes Gabby. (Cindy drops her purse during this business and Greg, who has entered near the end of the group picks it up and wanders off behind the trees.)

GWEN

Oo-oo an insect just landed on me. Someone get it off!

(All the girls are screaming and getting grossed out, except Diane; John comes over excitedly and nabs the bug.)

JOHN

(inspecting his specimen) Oh my, another bug for my collection. (talking to himself) That makes... let's see... 2147 and 1/2... since Harry's left wing fell off.

GWEN

(intrigued and disgusted) My goodness, what a slimy creature.

JOHN

No, they're not slimy. They're interesting, see? (He holds the bug right in front of her face and she runs off screaming. Arty, Lance, Gallager, and Rob step in front of Gwen protectively and walk threateningly towards John.)

ARTY

(nose to nose with John) Bug off, John.

ALEX

(slapping her thigh and laughing) "Bug off"... ha, ha, what a joker you are, Arty.

MR. DILL

(stepping between Arty and John) O.K. everyone! Get over here and make it fast! (everyone assembles) Now set up the tents. (Arty puts his arm around Gwen's neck and starts off to one side) Wait! Guys set up to my right and girls to my left.

STUDENTS

Aw-w. (Arty lets go of Gwen, kisses her hand, bows and goes off with the guys.)

MR. DILL

I'm going to help the bus driver find a suitable place to park and I expect you all to be done by the time I get back. (He exits.)

KATHY

Be careful of my designer Northface tent. It's extremely expensive.

DAN

(disgusted) What's your problem?

KATHY

Problem?

DAN

I don't see why you have to brag about
everything!

CINDY

Well... at least she has things to brag about
doesn't she? (She stares at him cruelly and he
storms off.)

GABBY

(jabbing Alex in the ribs) Oo-oo-oo did you see
his sleeping bag?

ALEX

(singing and dancing) His shirt is red, his pants
are blue. Where does he shop? Hee hee hoo
hoo.

DIANE

(elbowing Alex to stop) Knock it off, Alex. (with
authority) Come on, "ladies", I'll show you how
to set up a tent.

GWEN

(amazed) You know how to set up a tent?

DIANE

Of course, my family and I have travelled all
over the world in tents.

(Girls exit gossiping among themselves.)

MERLE

(looking around) This is a mystical place. A
place where anything could happen.

LANCE

(rubbing his shoulders and looking around)
Yah, like rain or snow or even hail.

SCOTT

(stealing back and forth among the trees)
Good, I like things cold.

GREG

(stepping out from behind a tree) Yah, like cold cash, maybe? (moving his brow up and down and leering)

GALLAGER

What are you doing back there, Greg?

GREG

Looking for my cabin.

ARTY

We're sleeping in tents, Greg. Where do you think we are, the Holiday Inn?

GALLAGER

(highbrow) The Holiday Inn?? You can't be serious. It's the Broadmoor (an expensive Colorado hotel) or nothing.

ROB

(worried) But I don't want to sleep out in a tent.

(The guys ad lib simultaneously about the merits of different hotels they've stayed in versus camping out.)

ROB

(aside) Nobody ever listens to me.

BUZZ

(entering with a brown paper bag from which she takes a sip) Uh... excuse me... does anybody know uh... where... I... uh... parked the... uh... bus?

ROB

Oh no... we're doomed!

CINDY

(running on with others) What's going on?

DAN

(ominously) You're doomed.

CINDY

What?

BUZZ

(sitting down and starting to cry) I lost the bus...

MR. DILL

(approaching) There you are, Buzz. I moved the bus to a more level spot, I hope you don't mind.

BUZZ

(exasperated) Mind?! I thought I was losing my mind.

MERLE

Too late for that I'm afraid.

DIANE

(wandering down stage) Hey look, you guys. This trail looks exactly like a path I saw on our travels through England. Yah, and this real old guy I meet there told me this great Medieval story... wanna hear it?

(Everyone ad libs their own quick response like, "not particularly" or "sure" or "I think I hear someone calling", depending on their character. Mr. Dill raises his voice over the crowd.)

MR. DILL

Be seated everyone. (Several people moan, with Cindy's and Arty's among the loudest.)Show some respect or I'll whack you one. (He slaps a stick he's holding into his hand near Cindy.)

CINDY

(pathetically) Mr. Dill, I already have a headache.

KATHY

Didn't you take some aspirin?

CINDY

I can't find my purse.

MR. DILL

(impatiently) All right! All of you, just sit down and listen to Diane's story. (He cracks his stick next to Arty.)

ARTY

(jumping) Okay, okay... we'll be cool.

MR. DILL

You better. Now, start, Diane. (He motions to Diane, who sits on the tree stump while everyone else settles in to listen. Cindy is still looking for her purse.)

DIANE

(mysteriously) Let me tell you about this path I saw. It was in a forest. A dark green forest with lots of trees overhead. It was so quiet you could hear water dripping from the morning dew left on the flowers.

JOHN

Were there any insects on these flowers?

ALEX

(silly) Stop it, John, you're "bugging" me.

(People start laughing and talking and not paying attention.)

CINDY

Has anyone seen my purse?

(Mr. Dill stands up and stares down at everyone in a menacing fashion.)

CINDY

(timidly) But I need some aspirin.

MERLE

(holding out two pills) Here, take this.

CINDY

What is it?

MERLE

A little something I whipped up in my lab.

BUZZ

(with interest) Got any more of them thingies?

MR. DILL

(snatching the pills from him) Give those to me!

MERLE

I was just kidding... it's aspirin.

(Mr. Dill examines the pills closely and then gives them to Cindy, clears his throat, gestures towards Diane and she resumes her storytelling.)

DIANE

Anyway, as I walked on this trail I did not know where it would lead. I felt like I was being watched, but saw no one.

CINDY

(under her breath) My purse is still missing.

MR. DILL

(cracking the stick) Quiet!

DIANE

Now legend has it, this trail was often used by knights, returning from their crusades, loaded with riches. These knights were targets for thieves, who found the dark forest an ideal place to hide. Without warning they would fiercely attack the knights, knocking them unconscious with clubs... (Lance and Gallager start having a mock fight with sticks, slashing it out over people, rocks, and in and out among the trees.)

MR. DILL

(pursuing them in the background) All right you two!

CINDY

(standing up and staring at everyone) Somebody stole my purse!

KATHY

Are you sure?

CINDY

Positive.

KATHY

(pointing to Dan, Scott, and John) All right, which one of you stole Cindy's purse?

JOHN

What would I need a purse for?

SCOTT

You probably lost it.

DAN

Yah. We didn't steal your stupid designer purse.

CINDY

Then where is it?

GABBY, KATHY, GWEN, AND ANNA

Yah, where is it?

ARTY

(He stands up and approaches the three guys with Rob nervously backing him up.) Hand it over guys, right now, or...

MR. DILL

(bringing Lance and Gallager down stage)Okay, that's it! (He lets the two go in front of him and quickly gets out the stick he had stashed through his belt loop.)

CINDY

Wait! (She steps between the guys as Mr. Dill raises his stick and accidentally hits Cindy, who falls into Arty and Dan's hands, unconscious. At this point there is a blackout, followed by strobe lights and some whirling music as characters rush off to make simple costume changes to suggest medieval dress. If characters in scene 1 have worn basic clothing, then they could have tunics or long skirts pulled over; it will go fairly quickly.)

Scene 2

(Diane is dressed pretty much gypsy-like throughout the play and now ties a scarf or some other adornment on and speaks as she moves to one edge of the stage in a follow spot light pool. The music quiets as she speaks but the background lights continue to whirl around.)

DIANE
The sheriff, in his rage to calm the thieves' attack and protect the royal party and attending ladies, wielded his sword hastily and accidentally knocked the lady Cynthia unconscious. (the strobe speeds up) Her world began spinning around and around... colors flashed (colored lights go on and off) she passed in and out of a land of shadow and light... mysterious and fantastic... full of strange sounds (the music is over-scored by strange sounds) and then suddenly... silence... (As the sounds abruptly end and the lights return to normal, we see Cynthia lying on the ground, with her head against a rock, and dressed as a well-to-do young woman of medieval times.) Suddenly she awoke alone in the forest and soon realized something strange and mysterious had happened to her in the moments that had passed.

CYNTHIA
(loudly moaning and rubbing her head) Ohhh...

QUEEN
(entering from one side and addressing the king) Darling, did you hear something?

KING
(looking off in a distracted manner) What...?

QUEEN
(stomping her foot angrily) I know I heard something and don't tell me I didn't!

KING
I believe you darling, so calm down. (pats her shoulder)

QUEEN

I am calm!

KING

You must not worry so much about the treasure.

(Three knights enter, set the treasure down, and stand at attention ready for orders.)

QUEEN

Sir Lancelot, Sir Gallahad, and Soon-to-be-Sir Robin-- I order you to find out who made that noise. And if it was thieves... off with their heads!

KNIGHTS

(taking out their swords, bowing, and jabbing each other by mistake as they do so) Yes, Your Ladyship.

(The knights blunder about looking for the source of the noise as Anastasia, Gabriel, and Katherine enter in a tussle.)

QUEEN

Anastasia! Please come over here... and bring Gabriel and Katherine with you. It's not safe in these woods.

ANASTASIA

(breaking up a squabble between the other two ladies) Gabriel, Katherine, the Queen would like to see us.

GABRIEL AND KATHERINE

(breaking off the tussle and curtsying low)Certainly.

CYNTHIA

(slowly sitting up and moaning in pain) Ohhhh...

(Merlin, the wizard, and Alexia, the joker, enter as Cynthia moans and Alexia screams and jumps into his arms. When she screams the ladies do also, scaring the knights who bump into each other. Lord Greg enters, taking in the scene, and Diana joins them to one side, as cool as a cucumber.)

ALEXIA

What was that noise, Diana?

DIANA

Probably just the wind... or perhaps...

ALL

Yes??

DIANA

...Spirits...?

(Everyone screams again and runs into each other. The king shouts above the din.)

KING

Silence everyone! (everyone freezes in a silly stage picture) Merlin! Look through your crystal ball.

MERLIN

(pulling out his crystal with everyone gathering around him) Oh crystal ball, I ask with poise, who's the maker, of that noise?

CYNTHIA

Ohhh...

(While everyone is spellbound from the elaborate movements Merlin made while consulting his ball, he slips away, finds Cynthia, and stands on the rock above her head.)

MERLIN

(hands outstretched triumphantly) The Lady Cynthia is making that noise, your Lordship.

THE ROYAL PARTY

(running up, gathering around Cynthia, and talking all at once) Cynthia? What's wrong? What happened? Are you hurt? Who is responsible for this deed?

(Lord Gregory slips away from the group, opens the treasure, and starts pocketing riches.)

GREGORY

(aside) This will be so easy. They will never miss a few gold pieces and maybe even a ruby or two... (He is disturbed by two thieves sneaking up and he turns to join the group gathered around Cynthia, but keeps an eye on the vagabonds.)

JONATHAN AND SCOTTON
(stage whisper) There it is, in the sack.

GREGORY
(hoping to get the king's attention on the thieves at the sack) You. You thieves, stop that at once!

JONATHAN AND SCOTTON
(recognizing Gregory) I thought we had a bargain!

GREGORY
(smiling wickedly at them) I've never seen you before in my life.

SCOTTON
Liar!

GREGORY
(hoping to incriminate the thieves) Your Highness! Come at once!

SCOTTON
(not understanding why Gregory, an accessor to many of their crimes, is turning on them) We'll get you for this!

JONATHAN
(grabbing Scotton and running off with him) Come on, Scotton!

GREGORY
(finally getting the king's attention and pointing to the empty treasure sack) Your Highness!

KING
(coming down and picking up the empty treasure sack) The treasure?... Missing?

QUEEN
What?! (running over to him followed by the knights)

CYNTHIA
What? (trying to stand)

GABRIEL

Lie down, Cynthia.

KATHERINE

You have a bump on your head.

ANASTASIA

We'll go and find out what has happened. You just lie here.

CYNTHIA

Yes, please, just leave me alone.

(The three ladies gather around the royal party, who are huddled around the empty sack arguing quietly. Delvar, the assassin, slips through the trees in the background, grabs Cynthia, holds a mock weapon to her, and begins pulling her off.)

CYNTHIA

Who are you? What do you want?

DELVAR

Never mind, you're coming with me.

CYNTHIA

(struggling as he starts off with her) Where are you taking me?

DELVAR

You'll find out. (he pulls her off)

QUEEN

(loudly) Well who could have taken it?

MERLIN

I shall consult my mystic powers. (stands in front of everyone and starts chanting)

KING

(noticing Cynthia's disappearance) Where has Cynthia gone?

GREGORY

(seeing another opportunity for incrimination) Surely you cannot think the Lady Cynthia has anything to do with the missing treasure?

KATHERINE

(distraught) I cannot believe it! My very best friend... a thief!

QUEEN

After Her! After her at once, my fine men! We cannot let her get away. (The knights start off, but all go crashing into each other as they stop when the king calls out.)

KING

Wait! We must find the sheriff at once. He will help us find her.

QUEEN

But where has he gone?

KING

He was clearing the forest of thieves and assassins before we passed through.

GREGORY

Little did he know the thief was among us all along.

KING

Enough! Be off. (holding his sword before him)

(They all exit except Diana, who continues the story.)

DIANA

So the lady Cynthia was wrongfully accused of stealing the kingdom's newly won treasure, while Lord Gregory carefully disappeared from the royal company. (Gregory has hung back from the group and now creeps through the forest heading the opposite direction.) Soon the sheriff had been found and many brave men assembled to help him search for Cynthia.

Scene 3

(Meanwhile the royal party has entered from the opposite side, following the sheriff, who stands upon the rock waving a quarter staff. Diana joins the group.)

SHERIFF
Hear ye, hear ye... the King has organized a search party to find the thief. (He slams the stick down on the word "thief", smashing it onto his own toe. He jumps off the rock, hopping around in pain and trips over the jester's wand.)

ALEXIA
(laughing hysterically) Hath thee a nice trip?

SHERIFF
Away, fool!

ALEXIA
Very well... see thee next fall (laughing again and doing a front shoulder roll prat fall)

KING
(raising his voice impatiently) Let us depart!

GALLAHAD
We shall prevail! (raises his sword and runs off)

ROBIN
(scared) I hope... (following Gallahad)

LANCELOT
Long live the Queen!

(Lancelot kisses the queen's hand, she smiles, and the king clears his throat breaking off their moment. The others follow the knights off. Alexia and Merlin start off, but stop, hear some voices on the other side, and hide behind the trees. Soon Buzzly, Jonathan, and Scotton enter.Buzzly carries on a large pot and cooking spoon and Scotton paces back and forth while Jonathan catches flies and eats them.)

SCOTTON
(angrily turning to Buzzly) Where is Lord Gregory?!

BUZZLY

(cackling) I don't know, why would you ask me? (tastes what's in the pot with the spoon, slurping loudly)

SCOTTON

Cuz we can't find him, ya old hag! (She takes her spoon and smacks him.)

BUZZLY

(straightening out her apron and going back to sampling her pot) Why are you looking for Lord Gregory anyway?I mean what would a noble lord like him be doin' with the likes of you?

JONATHAN

(popping a fly in his mouth) He's got the bootie.

ALEXIA

(stage whisper to Merlin) Why would he want a smelly old baby sock?

MERLIN

Doth thou not know the difference between thy infant clothing and stolen treasure?

BUZZLY

(whirling around) Who said that?

ALEXIA

(still hiding) We did.

SCOTTON

(holding out his knife and shouting) Show yourselves!

MERLIN

Very well. (They step out from behind the trees and walk down to the others.)

SCOTTON

Who are you?

JONATHAN

(circling around Merlin) What are you?

MERLIN

Merlin, the magician... here with a message from King Arthur.

BUZZLY

What about her? (to Alexia)

ALEXIA

Alexia, court jester. (She does a trick.)

BUZZLY

Oh-h. Buzzly Needsmore (curtsies) collector of odds and ends.

JONATHAN

A thief, you mean. (laughing)

BUZZLY

(chasing them all over with her spoon) You should talk, boys.

DIANA

(entering suddenly and crashing into the chase) Have you heard the news?! The bootie has been stolen and Lady Cynthia will hang for it!

SCOTTON

What? Lady Cynthia?

DIANA

Cynthia is suspected of stealing the royal bootie!

MERLIN

(deflated) So much for the royal message.

ALEXIA

Have any of you seen her?

BUZZLY

Can't say that we have.

DIANA

You must give it back, Scotton. I'll see that the king gets it and Cynthia is cleared of all false accusations.

JONATHAN

We don't have it. Lord Gregory took it. We're sure of it. He was supposed to create a diversion so we could steal it and then meet us here later to divvy up, but he double-crossed us.

SCOTTON

The lady was nowhere near it. In fact, she was knocked out on the ground.

ALEXIA

What a royal mess. (She laughs herself silly, Buzzly slaps her with the spoon, looks at her contorted expression, and then the both of them laugh hysterically.)

DIANA

Stop it! There's a search party out to find her and they're headed this way!

SCOTTON

(running his hands through his hair and pacing again) Why would she have run off? Where could she be?

MERLIN

(putting his hands to his head mysteriously) I can feel it... she is very near...

ALEXIA

(holding back a laugh) In other words, who knows? (She slaps Merlin on the back and sends him reeling forward.)

SCOTTON

Well let's find the real culprit, Lord Gregory.

JONATHAN

Aye! (starting off) Let's get him.

MERLIN

Wait, I'll go with you! (running after them)

ALEXIA

What about me? (following with a hop and a skip)

(Delvar enters from the other side and shoves Cynthia on. Diana rushes to her and gives her a hug.)

DIANA

Oh, Cynthia, there you are!

CYNTHIA

That vermon kidnapped me!

BUZZLY

(shaking her head and clicking her tongue in disapproval) Delvar, why'd ya do that?

DELVAR

Awhile back I heard her and her too-good lady friends making fun of me. I told her she would pay for the ill tempered remarks and now she's going to.

BUZZLY

Oh. (hands him the kettle) Here, have some soup.

DELVAR

Don't mind if I do. (slurping loudly) Buzzly, (amazed) this is good.

BUZZLY

Thanks.

DELVAR

(to Cynthia) Here have some.

CYNTHIA

I don't want anything from you.

BUZZLY

Well I'm afraid you're gonna get something from him anyway... something that even he didn't plan.

CYNTHIA

What are you talking about, beggar woman?

BUZZLY

You're to be hung.

DELVAR AND CYNTHIA

Hung?!

DIANA

You've been accused of taking the bootie.

CYNTHIA

(defensively) But I didn't take it.

BUZZLY
No, but it looks like ya did being as Delvar snatched you away just as the bootie was taken.

DELVAR
I-I... didn't know it would lead to this... I-I'm sorry, Cynthia... I just meant to scare you... teach you a lesson...

CYNTHIA
(hatefully) I bet you are.

(The search party can be heard offstage.)

DIANA
They're coming! Run! Hide!

(They scatter in all directions, but King Arthur's men block every exit.)

GALLAHAD
Halt there! The king awaits thee.

(Cynthia runs the other direction but finds it blocked)

LANCELOT
Surrender, Cynthia! You and your band of traitors are no match for the knights of the round table.

CYNTHIA
Band of traitors?I don't even know them, except for Diana, and she only came to warn me.

GALLAHAD
A likely story.

CYNTHIA
(to Delvar) And this man kidnapped me!

ROBIN
Fine excuses for a thief.

LANCELOT
Well if you deny they are your accomplices, you shall die alone.

DELVAR
(pulling out his sword) No, I will protect you!

(A large fight breaks out between Delvar and Lancelot and Gallahad. Buzzly fights Robin with her spoon and in the end Diana pours her soup over his head and Buzzly knocks him out. Delvar fights bravely, but in the end is run through and falls back in Cynthia's arms.)

GALLAHAD
(wiping his sword) Foolish man. Now we will seal your fate as well, Cynthia.

LANCELOT
One moment, Gallahad. (to Cynthia) Perhaps if you hand over the treasure immediately, the king will be merciful and throw you in the dungeon rather than hanging you.

CYNTHIA
(Attending Delvar's wound with Buzzly and Diana) But I don't have it.

LANCELOT
Then you must answer to the king!

(The king, queen and sheriff enter, followed by the ladies.)

KING
Relinquish the treasure!

CYNTHIA
But I don't have it, my Lord.

QUEEN
Traitor! She must hang!

CYNTHIA
But...

QUEEN
Silence! No excuses! Get the noose, Sir Robin.

ROBIN
Yes, my Lady! (he gets a rope ready)

KING
Sheriff! Take her to the tree stump, blindfold her, and secure her wrists behind her.

SHERIFF
Yes, my Lord. (he pulls her away from Delvar)

CYNTHIA
How can you do this? You can't believe I
actually stole the treasure! Aren't you my
friends? Don't you believe me?

KATHERINE
A traitor to the throne is no friend of mine!

GABRIEL
Nor mine!

ANASTASIA
You've betrayed our family!

ROYAL PARTY
Hang her!

(By now she is standing on the stump bound and gagged. The rope should appear
to be around her neck, but in no way should be actually able to injure her if she
were to lose her balance.)

SCOTTON
(rushing on) Wait! She is not the thief!

JONATHAN
(entering with Gregory bound and gagged)
Here is your thief.

LANCELOT
Highway robbers!

GALLAHAD
Attack!

ROBIN
Not again.

(A wild fight breaks out between the knights, sheriff and thieves. The ladies are
running around hysterically. Buzzly and Diana get a few good licks in and the king
protects the queen. Suddenly Merlin and Alexia burst in. Thunder sounds and
Merlin freezes everyone in one huge ridiculous stage picture.)

MERLIN
Wait! Now look here. (everyone's eyes only
rivet towards him) Cynthia did not steal the
treasure. It was Lord Gregory, who apparently
suffers from an advanced state of kleptomania.

ALL
(still frozen) Klepto- what?

KING
Are you sure about all this?

MERLIN
Yes. He has been stealing from your Lordship for years. We found his secret hiding place and all your missing treasures.

ALEXIA
Naughty, naughty.

QUEEN
(in a particularly awkward pose) All right, we believe you. Please unfreeze us immediately.

MERLIN
I will as soon as I am sure that you will hand Lord Gregory over to me for immediate treatment.

KING
Treatment?

MERLIN
Yes... consisting of several spells, incantations, anti-klepto potions, and... if all else fails...

ALL
Yes??

MERLIN
I might have to resort to psychiatric therapy.

KING
Psychi-ahh- (getting flustered) Very well then, I agree. Release us from your magic, Merlin.

(Merlin waves his arms, mumbling incantations, thunder sounds, the lights flicker and Cynthia starts to lose her balance on the stump. Scotton and Jonathan rush to catch her in the confusion.)

KATHERINE
Oh no! Look! Cynthia is falling!

DELVAR
Get her!

KING
Quick! She'll hang herself!

(The strobe light comes on, everyone is talking at once and running off to quickly change back into contemporary dress. The strange whirling music comes up again and Diana walks toward the audience and then across the apron, taking off her medieval gypsy costume accessories as she continues to tell the story.)

DIANA

She dangled from the rope for just a moment. Though those around rushed to her aide, she quickly lost consciousness... she drifted into darkness... (the stage darkens) she was falling... falling... (a spotlight light cuts through the darkness) Suddenly there was light from the darkness... a tunnel of light... she was drawn towards it... at the last moment she was pulled back... (the light goes out and the actors assemble around Cindy, who is lying on her back near where Mr. Dill had accidentally hit her in scene 1.) Above her towered faces, all shouting at the same time... she felt like she couldn't breathe... (The lights slowly come up.)

Scene 4

CINDY

(choking)Help!!

ALL

(ad libbing simultaneously) I hope she's all right. What is it? Wake up, Cindy! She's off in the ozone...

MR. DILL

(to Lance and Gallager) If you two hadn't been messing around none of this would have happened.

LANCE

We said we're sorry!

GALLAGER

What do you want, blood?

BUZZ

Well... if that's what you wanted, you got it!

GABBY

She's bleeding!

MR. DILL

(to Scott) Here, hold this hankie on her head. Buzz and I will go get the first aide kit from the bus.

BUZZ

Sure thing, cutie. (They run off together.)

CINDY

(sitting up and trying to loosen the necktie she is wearing) Get this noose off of me!

ANNA

She's delirious!

SCOTT AND JOHN

Here, let us help you. (taking her necktie off)

KATHY

(snobbish) Would you leave her alone, she doesn't like you.

CINDY

(dazed) No, no, it's all right.

ARTY

(yelling from the far side of the group) Leave her alone you creeps! (pushes Dan out of the way and then Gallager, Lance and Robin pull Scott and John up and away from Cindy)

CINDY

(standing up and holding the hankie to her head) Shush up, Arty. They're my friends!

KATHY

You must of had a real bad dream thinking they're your friends.

CINDY

Oh be quiet, you snob!

KATHY

(taken aback) Snob?! (near tears) But just an hour ago we were the best of friends!

CINDY

Not any more!

SCOTT

(questionably) An hour ago you didn't want to talk to us.

DAN

Yah, why are we your friends now?

JOHN

Yah?

LANCE

(grabbing John's shoulder) Don't get your hopes up, reknob!

CINDY

(walking forward dreamily) It all has to do with my dream.

ALL

Dream?

MERLE
That must have been some dream!

GWEN
So what about your dream?

CINDY
(confused) I don't know... it was really realistic,
though... (taking the hankie from her head and
sitting on the rocks reflectively)

DAN
Well... um.... what was your dream about?

ALL
Yah, Cindy, what was your dream about?

CINDY
Well...

(Mr. Dill and Buzz enter carrying the first aid kit. Buzz is surprised that Cindy is up
and her head has stopped bleeding.)

BUZZ
Well I guess you're all right, aren't ya', honey?

CINDY
Just a slight headache is all.

DIANE
Did you ever take those aspirin?

CINDY
(opening her hand and feeling embarrassed)
No...

ALEX
(giggling) Oh, Cindy, you're such a clown.

MR. DILL
Well now, here's a canteen of water. Why don't
you sit down, take your aspirin, let Buzz put a
bandage on your head, and listen while Diane
finishes her story.

GALLAGER
Oh come on man, Cindy was about to tell us
about her dream.

MR. DILL

(clearing his throat and staring at Gallager) A-
hem.

GALLAGER

(laughing awkwardly) Okay, you guys, come
on. Mr. Dill (whispering) Pickle (normal volume)
wants us to listen to the rest of the story. (sits
down in front of Diane and folds his hands in a
mocking example of perfect student behavior)

MR. DILL

Watch it, young man.

GALLAGER

Yes, sir.

GABBY

Would you zip it up, Gallager, it's a good story.

CINDY

It's okay, guys, my story can wait.

MERLE

Let's hear it, little spirit!

(Alex breaks up laughing, but Mr. Dill gives her the evil eye.)

DIANE

Let's see... and then she found that the thieves,
peasants, and commoners she had scorned for
years, weren't really that bad.

ALEX

(bursting out laughing again) They weren't
huh? What were they, saints?

BUZZ

Sh-h-h, you just interrupted the story!

ALEX

(quietly) Oh... sorry...

DIANE

Are you guys sure you want me to finish the
story?

ALL

(ad libbing) Sure. Go on. Yah. Go ahead.

DIANE

And then she found out that they weren't so bad. Because it was those commoners who came to her defense, took the rope from her neck and rescued her. And from that day forward, she had friends among the nobles as well as friends among the commoners. She found that at whatever level of life people lived... no matter if they're rich or poor... from good homes or bad... people are people... no one is better than anyone else.

ALEX

(laughing again)That was so-o-o funny.

MR. DILL

No it wasn't.

BUZZ

What a screwball kid.

CINDY

(standing) Wait, you guys! That was just like my dream!

MERLE

Deja' vu!

GREG

(clearing his throat) By the way, Cindy, here's your purse. It somehow got tangled in my gear.

ALL

(turning and staring at Greg) Sure it did!

(There is a blackout and then the curtain closes in the darkness.)

(This play is an example of one written with historic and social science themes addressed. Students wanted to look at class systems, materialism, prejudice, crime and punishment. In addition to that, they wanted to explore fantasy, comedy, and especially physical comedy. Choosing a forest as a setting, gave them a timeless place, one that often is the host for tales of old. They also had lights and a sound system available, so that's in their stage directions, but of course it could be done much more simply.)

BIBLIOGRAPHY

Doll, Ronald C. Curriculum Improvement Decision Making andProcess. New York: Allyn and Bacon, Inc., 1986.

National Middle School Association. This We Believe. Georgia: Panaprint Inc., 1982.

Polsky, Milton E. You Can Write A Play. New York: The Rosen Publishing Company, 1983.

Siks, Geraldine B. Drama With Children. New York: Harper and Row Publishing Company, 1977.

Smiley, Sam. PlaywritingThe Structure of Action. NewJersey: Prentice-Hall, Inc., 1971.

Spolin, Viola. Improvisation for the Theater A Handbook ofTeaching and Directing Techniques. Illinois: Northwestern University Press, 1977.

Stein, Jess. The Random House Dictionary. New York: Random House, Inc., 1980.

Tanner, Fran A. Basic Drama Projects. Idaho: Clark Publishing Company, 1972.

Made in the USA
Lexington, KY
23 September 2018